Danger

(Fletcher Pratt and Irvin Lester)

Kartindo Publishing House (Kartindo.com)

The wind rose in the night and by dawn the sky was streaming with torn and ragged masses of cloud moving from south to north like an army in flight. There was a shiver of cold in the air and the seas ran so high that effective work was impossible, so we gathered in Professor Hartford's cabin to help the old man brave out his discomfort by getting him to talk. The way in which he kept up his spirit, if not his body, through all the miseries of seasickness on that trip, was one of the finest exhibitions of courage I have seen anywhere.

As the senior member of the Museum's staff he was, in a sense, in charge of the expedition, though like the rest of us, he was inclined to let things run themselves while he pursued his specialty. Perhaps it was fortunate for him that the protozoa can be studied as well on a constantly moving steamer as on dry land; for the work kept his mind off his troubles. At all events, every day that was calm enough for him to be out of bed, found him poring over his microscope in search of hitherto undescribed forms

Kartindo Publishing House (Kartindo.com)

in this remote corner of the Pacific.

On days such as this he lay in his bunk, and between uneasy heavings of the mal-de-mer that plagued him, lectured our crowd of assorted scientific experts on the importance of unicellular life. Very interesting lectures they must have been to the other chaps; even I was sometimes caught by the spell of the professor's keen and philosophical observation, and as a mere artist I always felt more or less a misfit among all those -ologies and -isms.

I remember this day in particular, partly because the evening brought us to our first view of Easter Island and partly because the conversation turned to those scientific generalizations; which are both easier to understand and more interesting to the non-scientific hearer. But even then, I probably would have recalled it only as one of a number of similar talks, had not after events given it a peculiar, almost a sinister significance.

Burgess, our entomologist, had been trying to draw the professor out by descanting on the rising tide of insect life. "Sooner or later," he declared, "we will

Kartindo Publishing House (Kartindo.com)

have to fight for our lives with them. Science always
plods along behind their attacks. They have taken
the chestnut, the boll-weevil and corn-borer are
taking two more of our economically important
plants. Who knows but that nature is working in its
slow way to send us after the dinosaurs?"

Slap, slap, went the waves against the cabin wall.

"Perhaps, perhaps," mused Professor Hertford,
"though I incline to think that the insects will never
drive man from the planet. Evolution allows a group
only one opportunity--the insects had their chance to
rule the world in the Carboniferous, and failed.

"... No," he went on, "there are many lines of
evolution untried, but none of them lead through
existing forms. When a more capable type than man
appears, it will be in a wholly new form of animal
life--perhaps even a direct evolution from the
protozoa. So far as we know, evolution along that
line has never taken place to any great extent. The
division between the one-celled and many-celled
animals is sharper than that between an insect and an
elephant. Think of a one-celled animal, practically

immortal as they are and possessed of intelligence. No matter what work we do, no matter what records we leave, the greater portion of human knowledge perishes with the minds that give it birth. Think what it would mean if one person could go on gathering knowledge through the centuries."

"But," objected Burgess, "a parmoecium hasn't any brain tissue. You can't have that without some nervous organization."

"But, my dear Burgess," said the professor, urbanely, "is brain tissue necessary to thought? You might as well say fins are necessary to swimming. Neither the polar bear nor the octopus have them, yet both can swim very well. Nature has a queer way of accomplishing similar results by all sorts of different means. Suppose thought is what Osborn hints it is--a matter of chemical reaction, and interaction--is there any need for brain tissue in which the thought must take place?"

"All true enough," said Burgess, "but you must admit that without proprioceptors there can be no sensation, and with a cortex--"

Kartindo Publishing House (Kartindo.com)

The conversation became so technical that I was perforce eliminated from it, and wandered down the iron stairway to watch the engines. For a time I sat there, vainly trying to put on paper the flicker of those bright moving parts--so beautifully ordered, so Roman in their efficient performance of their task, whatever else was happening. But it was no use; a job for a Nevinson, and I clambered back to the deck.

There I found the weather had moderated. The whole southwest was streaked with the orange presage of a fairer day and, right in the center of the illumination, grey and ominous, a huge cone rose steeply from the water.

"That's Puakatina," said Bronson the mate, pausing beside me. "There's an anchorage right beneath it, but we'll have to work round to the west of Cook's Bay to get shelter from the wind. I was here on a guano ship ten years ago. Damndest place you ever saw--no water, no fish, no nothing."

Morning found us at anchor in the bay and already scattering to our several pursuits. For me, Easter

Kartindo Publishing House (Kartindo.com)

Island was a fairyland. Never, among primitive work, have I seen such sculpture. It far surpassed the best Egyptian work, for every one of those cyclopean heads was a portrait, and almost a perfect one. I cannot better express my feeling for them than by saying that now, as I am writing this account with the memory sharp in my mind, of she strange and terrible events that took place later, I must still turn aside to pay tribute to those statues.

After all they are not so far from my story. Indeed, it was the statues that gave me what should have been a clue--a queer idea that all was not quite as it should be on this island--an idea that I would dismiss as an afterview, were it not that I find on the margin of one of my sketches, made at the time, a note to the effect that something very curious must have happened on the island. Those stones were carved by nothing less than a race of conquerors, with stern high faces, utterly different from the easy-going Polynesians of today. What became of them?

The same impression, of some weird catastrophe, was confirmed by other members of the expedition.

Kartindo Publishing House (Kartindo.com)

There were almost no fish, very little life for the botanists to chew on, and Hertford announced at one of our cabin conferences that the waters, as Agassiz had reported, were quite devoid of plankton. He pooh-poohed the idea of the subsidence of a large land put forth by De Salza, our geologist. "Subsidence," he said, "would leave the plankton and fish untouched. It is more as though some destructive organism had swept every trace of life from the locality. All the birds and the few fish are obviously recent immigrants, like the people."

Despite my entreaties for more time to make sketches, the scientists had done about all they could with this barren land in a week or so, and we hauled up anchor for Sala-y-Gomez, three hundred miles further east, taking a couple of the islanders with us. In spite of its atmosphere of ruin and gloom I was sorry to leave Easter Island, but there was the possibility that Sala-y-Gomez might contain some traces of the Easter script or carvings, and I felt it necessary to refuse Hertford's offer to leave me and stop on the way back.

Kartindo Publishing House (Kartindo.com)

Upon Sala-y-Gomez too, we came just at evening, marking it by the white line of foam along its low-lying shores as we felt our way slowly among the reefs, and here occurred another of those trivial incidents which are straws pointing in the direction of hidden things.

I was standing by the rail with Howard, the icthyological man, idly watching the wires of the dredge where they interrupted the slow curls of water turned back by our bow when there was a heavy muffled clang, and we saw the lines of the dredge tighten to tensity. Howard signalled for it to be drawn in, and together we watched the big scoop, eager to see what it had encountered. To our surprise it held only a little sea-weed.

"Now that's odd," said Howard, searching the sea-weed, with a small hand glass. "I could have sworn that dredge caught something heavy."

"It did," I answered, pointing. There was a long scratch of bright metal along one side.

"Corals possibly," he remarked. "Hey, Bronson, any

Kartindo Publishing House (Kartindo.com)

reefs charted here?"

The mate strolled up. "Not on the charts," he said, "but you never can tell. These Chilean charts aren't very good, you know."

"M-m-m" murmured Howard, continuing his examination. "There ought to be fragments of coralline formation here, but there aren't. Wonder what is could have been? Almost as though we'd caught something and it got away."

The thought of Hertford's comment about a destructive organism slipped into my mind, to be dismissed as not worth mentioning. Rock, shark, almost anything would have made that mark on the dredge.

There were no specimens ready to be sketched in the morning, and I went ashore with the first boat to wander about the island with my drawing materials. It must have been nearly noon when I rounded a jutting outcrop of rock to see before me a little sandy cove, placid and unresponsive in the heat, without a sign of life. Far ahead, a dark blob of rock was the

Kartindo Publishing House (Kartindo.com)

only mark on the perfect line of the beach. It was so suavé a scene that I sat down to make a sketch. After I had pencilled it in and was mixing the brown color for the cliffs, I noted that the rock seemed to have moved, but I attributed it to imagination and went on with my coloring. It must have been quite ten minutes when I looked up again. This time there could be no doubt--neither the outline nor the position of the rock were at all as I had recorded them.

In some excitement, I started to climb down the cliff toward this singular rock that changed place and form, but the distance was considerable, and while I was still a quarter of a mile away, it moved again, visibly this time, sliding down to the water's edge, where it disappeared beneath the gentle surge. The most peculiar thing about it was that there seemed to be no sensible method of progress; it flowed, like a huge, irregular drop of liquid.

I hurried back to the camp with my sketch and my tale, but found the rest in no condition to listen. Old Makoi Toa, one of the Easter Islanders we had

Kartindo Publishing House (Kartindo.com)

brought along with us, had been killed, apparently by a snake. "He was fishing down the beach ahead of the rest," said Howard, "just out of sight beyond that rock. We all heard him scream, and hurried to the spot. When we got there he was already dead, with a round hole in his chest, and shortly after he turned that hideous blue black that people turn to who die of snake-bite. It might have been one of those sea-snakes but for the size of the wound."

"I'm sure I saw something sliding away into the water," added Greaves, the botanist, "but it didn't look in the least like a snake."

The shadow of the old man's death lay on our little cabin conference that night, inhibiting speech, though the means of it remained a mystery. It was not until I told my tale that there was any conversation at all. As I finished there was a little moment of silence, during which each one made the obvious parallel between the occurrence and the death of Makoi Toa, and then Professor Hertford asked to see my sketch. He looked at it closely for a moment.

Kartindo Publishing House (Kartindo.com)

"Unless I am mistaken, gentlemen," he said, "we are facing an unknown organism of serious potentialities. May I ask that you do not go ashore to-morrow unless you are well armed and in pairs?"

"What is it, professor?" asked de Salza.

"I would prefer not to hazard a guess just yet. I may be in error." And that was the last word on the subject that we could draw from him, although de Salza laughed at the idea of anything sinister in connection with this little spot of land.

The next day was bright and clear, and after attending the burial service for Makoi Toa, I sought Greaves and together we made for the spot where I had seen the moving rock. I admit we were culpable in not going armed as the professor advised, but who would then have thought....?

We reached the place about the same time I had been there the previous day, climbed down the cliffs with each other's help, and walked across the white sand of the cove, to where I had seen the moving rock. It was not more than ten yards from the edge of a place where the receding tide of years had left a number of little arched caves. Just where I had sketched the rock was a ridge of sand pulled aside by the weight of whatever had been there, and in the center of it, a round, bard ball, perhaps three or four inches in diameter. Greaves picked it up, turning it over curiously.

"Why, it's feathers and bones," he said, extending if to me, "just as though it had been regurgitated by a pelican or an eagle after a meal."

I reached my hand for it, and just then, by the grace of Providence, caught a flicker of motion out of the tail of my eye. I turned to meet it; my foot gave on the soft sand, and I fell prone. It was the fall that saved me for something sharp whistled not an inch past my shoulder as I went down. The next instant I heard Greaves shout, and felt him tug my arm, and in the same moment something cold and clammy and hard grated and gripped against my foot. A horrible fear, the fear of imminent death, turned me to ice; I seemed incapable of movement, but somehow got to one knee, and between my own efforts and Greaves' pull, the grip on my foot relaxed. I half stumbled, half-rolled down the sand, and as I did so, there was another whistling flash and something struck the pocket of my coat, going right through the cloth and the sketch pad beneath it, to fall short of my skin by the narrowest of margins. Greaves was pulling me to my feet, and in a moment we were running.

In the interests of science I regret that we stood not on the order of our going. Neither of us spoke till we turned and paused at the top of the cliff, after a breathless climb. The cove was as empty as it had been before.

"My God--What was it?" I gasped.

"I don't know, I don't know." Greaves was half sobbing with excitement. "Something big and sort of--all soft--threw those things at us--half a dozen of the them--My God."

We were both so much shaken that the journey back to the camp seemed interminable, and it was some time after our arrival before a consecutive story

Kartindo Publishing House (Kartindo.com)

could be gotten out of Greaves. When he did tell his tale, it appeared that he had noticed the thing almost as soon as I--a great, dead brown object of uncertain form which had slid up softly from the water and shot out the darts I had seen without warning or sound, "as a cuttlefish does when you touch it," said Greaves, with a shudder. "The horrible part about it was that the thing had no eyes but seemed to see perfectly and know just where to move to head us off. I thought I'd never get you pulled loose... All the time I was dodging those darts I kept thinking about Makoi Toa...."

"I think you will agree," said Professor Hertford, when he had finished his rather incoherent account, "that my anticipations have been realized. Everything points to the presence in these waters of an efficient and destructive organism, capable not only of dominating the whole animal environment, but possibly even of depopulating Easter Island. From your description which is very rough and inaccurate, I should not be surprised to find it a giant new species of infusorian of jellyfish. Both types have those stinging tentacles. I am in favor of

Kartindo Publishing House (Kartindo.com)

remaining until we obtain more data about this animal, but as some--er--danger may attend such a course, I should prefer to leave it to the majority."

What could we do in the face of such an appeal? Personally, I had felt the grip on my foot and had no desire to feel it again. I could understand the flame of scientific interest driving the others, but it was rather with foreboding than enthusiasm that I listened to the eager plans they made for entrapping one of the animals which had attacked us.

I doubt whether anybody except de Salza (who was a human fish, intolerant of anything but the record of the rocks) was absent from the group which gathered behind the top of the cliffs the next morning to watch the fluttering antics of a chicken pegged out on the sand where we had met our adventure. Howard and Grimm (the conchologist) were armed with the only two rifles the expedition afforded, it having been agreed that it was better to examine a dead specimen before trying to take a live one.

The sun grew unconscionably hot as it swung across the sky. We conversed in low tones and were wondering whether we had come on a wild goose chase when I saw Howard beside me, stiffen to attention. I looked around--there was a break in the ripple, and through it slowly emerged the shape of the monster, dull brown in hue. I felt a quiver of excitement; the chicken was straining to the limit of its rope. There was a crack! that made all of us jump, as someone fired. "No, not yet," cried the professor, but the dark form took no notice, only moved on, formless and flowing, with half a score of short tentacles waving before it. Then it appeared to notice the chicken, paused, waved a tentacle or two at it, and there was a flicking motion as one of the darts shot out. The chicken went limp and the monster flowed gently over it. When it had passed, chicken, rope, and even the stake, were gone.

Both men were now firing, but they might as well have been throwing peas. The fantastic mound of jelly rolled back into the water in the same leisurely fashion it had come out, and disappeared.

Everybody began to talk at once, "The thing must be bullet proof!" "Invertebrate, but what an invertebrate!" "So that's what cleaned up Easter Island!" "Did you notice the ossicles?" "It's a hydroid!" "More like a medusid." "What do you think, Dr. Hertford?"

On one thing the conference that followed was agreed: that the animal, whatever it was, must be captured and examined. Various wild suggestions about dynamite and chemicals came up to be laughed down, and it was Dr. Hertford, as usual, who supplied the determining factor.

"It seems to me," said he, "that it would be worth while to postpone our trip to the continent and attempt to take one of these animals in one of the mammal cages. I believe the one you shot at was at least seriously injured; it seems incredible that it could be altogether bullet proof. We may, therefore, have a wall before another appears. What do you say?"

De Salza's was the only dissenting voice. I kept silence. I wish I had not, for though my protest might have done little good, it would at least have taken a load from my conscience that can never be quite clear now. However, I made no protest. The cage was rigged up on the shore with another chicken inside and a trick arrangement to slam the door shut on the invader and we sat down at the cove to wait.

It was the afternoon of the third day from the installation of the cage, and I was in my tent at the camp, trying to capture the color pattern of a small and very wiggly fish when the excited voice of Howard hailed us to announce that the cage held a prisoner. At once everything else was forgotten and we all hurried off, pell-mell, Dr. Hertford for all his years, well in the lead.

Sure enough the little mammal cage was filled to overflowing with the brown jelly-like mass of the monster, a tentacle or two waving in a friendly manner from the edges of the mass where it bulged between the bars. I admit it gave me a gone feeling in the pit of the stomach to watch it; it was like nothing I had ever seen or heard of, but among the scientists it produced only the liveliest interest.

Warned by previous experience, they approached it

Kartindo Publishing House (Kartindo.com)

with some caution, Howard carrying a piece of sheet iron from the ship before the professor like a shield-bearer in the days of the Iliad, while Greaves and Grimm came behind at a respectable distance, bearing rifles at the ready.

As they drew near, I heard the professor cry out in excitement, "Why, it's a protozoan! Look, the nucleus, and those cilia! And the triocysts! A single celled animal, by all that's holy! Related to Loxodes unless I am mistaken." Simultaneously, Greaves and Grimm, attracted by his words, drew a step nearer, and even Howard lowered the sheet iron to peer at the animal. And in that moment it happened.

With an indescribable swaying motion, the jelly-like mass in the cage seemed to surge through the narrow opening in the cage, and as it surged, the air about it was filled with the flash of those deadly darts. I heard Howard cry out, I saw Grimm leap; a gun was discharged, and the sheet iron clanged on the sand. Then there was silence and the brown mass in the cage oozed slowly across the sand to the four dead men, who writhed for a moment and lay still.

Kartindo Publishing House (Kartindo.com)

I think I must have gone a little mad in the next moments. I can never recall quite accurately what happened. I remember only a paralyzing mist of horror, and the walls of my cabin. They tell me that the cove was found utterly empty save for the cage with its door shut tight... I do not know... I do not know. A round ball, like the ball of feathers and bones found by Greaves was picked up later on the beach. It held shattered human bones, a fragment of blue cloth and a brass key, nothing more. I did not see it.

Even today, the memory of the horror of that moment gives me sleepless nights and days of shuddering. All too clearly I recall the words of that brave and gentle man who went to his death on the beach of Sala-y-Gomez, "When a type to replace man appears, it will be a direct evolution from the protozoa..." All too clearly, I remember his last words, and the desolation wrought by these animals on Easter Island and through that great stretch of the Eastern Pacific known as the Agassiz triangle, and I wonder how long it will be before they invade the continents.

Kartindo Publishing House (Kartindo.com)

It will be long, of that I am certain. The length of the time makes me wish to forget it and leave the future to care for itself. But I feel it a duty to the memory of Dr. Hertford to lay aside my own feeling. and place this story before the public, especially since de Salza, the only surviving member of that disastrous expedition, has cast doubt upon his conclusions and has disparaged his memory. If, in the face of a de Salza's reputation, I have succeeded in convincing even a few that humanity is on the verge of a battle to the death with a perhaps superior form of life, I am content; I have accomplished my purpose.

The End

Kartindo Publishing House (Kartindo.com)